A BORROWED ÁNGEL

Healing the heart after losing a child

Tahimy Peña Oliva

Rafael D. Tamayo Olivé

With love

Rafael y Tahimy Peug

Copyright © 2024 Tahimy Peña Oliva
Rafael D. Tamayo Olivé

Title: A BORROWED ANGEL
Subtitle: Healing the heart after losing a child

Size: 124 p.; 13,97 x 21,59 cm

ISBN: 9798310588899

Editing, design and layout:
Escuela de Autores
Fort Myers, Florida, 33905, U.S.A.
info@escueladeautores.com
🕾 13057078850
📞 (305)707-8850

ALL RIGHTS RESERVED
Any part of this book may be reproduced or stored in any electronic, mechanical, photocopying, memory storage or other system, or transmitted in any form or by any means.
ONLY WITH THE EXPRESS PERMISSION OF THE AUTHOR.

DEDICATION

I dedicate this book to our almighty God, who has given us, gives us, and will continue to give us strength at all times.

To Grandma Loida, who, even in Elón's final moments, reminded him of eternal truths that led him to make the best decision of his life: to follow Christ.

To all those who have lost a loved one, so they may find encouragement, comfort, and strength; and instead of focusing on the sorrow of death, may they cherish the beautiful gift of life.

ACKNOWLEDGMENTS

«*Not to us, O Lord, not to us, but to Your name give glory...*»

(Psalm 115:1a)

First, we thank our God for the blessing of allowing us to enjoy our son Elón for eleven precious years.

To all the brothers and sisters who have supported us with their prayers.

To those who have criticized us, as their observations have helped improve our perspective.

To the Gámez family, for standing by our side and informing the Convention, the pastors, and the congregation about what happened. Thank you so much!

To the Eastern Cuba Baptist Convention, for accompanying us and offering their support with their presence during this challenging time for our family.

ACKNOWLEDGMENTS

To the pastors who left their congregations to be with us.

To all the brothers and sisters from various denominations who joined us. The number of fellow servants present was so large that it is impossible to name each one individually. Thank you very much!

To the amazing editorial team God provided me. You have made the realization of this book possible—a long-cherished dream for our family. In Cuba: Dayamí, Junior, and Juan Pablo. In the United States: Débora Cornell, Loida Cornell, and ZwSalgado.

To the School of Authors, especially Professor Carlos Aparcedo and his team. All of you have made this dream come true, and I pray the Lord rewards your labor of love.

And to you, dear reader, we wish to be a blessing in the name of our Lord Jesus Christ. We pray that through these pages, He may provide comfort and that you may find the peace that surpasses all understanding.

TABLE OF CONTENTS

INTRODUCTION 11

Chapter 1
LITTLE DIAMONDS 13

Chapter 2
AN UNFORGETTABLE FAREWELL 45

Chapter 3
THE STAGES OF BEREAVEMENT OF A LOVED ONE 69

    The negotiation stage: I would do anything to change this situation 75

    The depression stage: Why continue after this loss? 77

    The acceptance stage: It's going to be fine. 80

    The guilt stage 84

    Different forms of parental grief 85

    How children and teenagers understand death 86

    Tips to help siblings cope with grief 87

    This will help free them from feelings of guilt and remorse. 88

    Helping yourself through grief 90

Chapter 4
TURNING OUR SORROWS INTO STRENGTHS 99
    An unexpected call 101
    A love letter from God 109
    A revealing dream 111
    Remember the following: 114

Bibliography 123

INTRODUCTION

May we be an instrument, like a sharp sword, able to penetrate your heart and work the miracle of a true and glorious transformation. May we be able to mitigate or soothe any pain you carry; change sadness into joy and turn your battles into victories. If we achieve this, we would feel fulfilled, though not entirely, because:

«So you also, when you have done all that you were commanded, say: We are unworthy servants; we have only done our duty.»

(Luke 17:10)

We long to be collaborators, like pencils in the hands of the Great Writer of history. Perhaps He has placed this book in your hands to add color to your life while making you a participant. We hope that, with your own shades, you can be used as a protagonist, like a brush in the hands of the Artist, the great Painter of humanity.

INTRODUCTION

Each battle is unique; and we, with ours, and you, with yours, share the same promise of victory. We can overcome!

«I can do all things through Christ who strengthens me.»

Stay Strong—you can do it!

Author: **Rafael Tamayo Olive**

Chapter 1
LITTLE DIAMONDS

I have titled this chapter «Little Diamonds» because I want to share with you some glimpses of our son Elón's life. These moments are like precious stones that God lent us, and I hope they will, in some way, help you get to know our story.

It was the year 1992, and the medical prognosis was discouraging. My fragile health made the idea of having children seem unlikely. At the time, a couple we were friends with had just welcomed their baby girl, and everyone kept saying, "*She looks just like her dad!*" I felt a deep ache in my heart because the doctors had told me it was improbable that I could ever give birth. I thought I would never be able to give Rafael that joy. For the first time, I directed a request to my Heavenly

Father: "God, if you were to give me a child, I ask that they look like their dad."

On March 18, 1993, in Las Tunas, Cuba, God answered my prayer with the arrival of Elón Tamayo Peña. He was beautiful and big: he weighed eight pounds and fourteen ounces, and he looked just like his dad! How grateful I was to the Lord for that child...

Elón was a miracle of God in every sense. At birth, he suffered fetal distress due to the presence of four meconium crosses. Meanwhile, the medical staff was running around attending to other mothers in critical situations. I then placed my hands on my belly and prayed: "Father, if this child is meant to be for You, make him be born. I want to be sure that he will bElóng to You completely."

My dear friend Lidia never left my side. After the delivery, she cried as she remembered how difficult it had been, but also how well God had cared for both of us.

When we left the hospital and were back home, I prayed again: «*Lord, from today I ask for Elón's future wife. I want her to love him as much as I love Rafa.*

Keep him pure and clean for You and for the wife You will give him; keep her as well.»

Ten months after his birth, while I was standing in front of his crib, I hugged my husband and shared my desire to have another baby. What a surprise it was to find out, less than a week later, that I was already expecting our second child! The promise from Isaiah 65:24 was fulfilled in my life: «Before they call, I will answer; while they are still speaking, I will hear.» We named our second son Isaí.

Elón means «Man of God» and Isaí means «*Servant of God.*» My heart's joy was immense as I watched them grow mischievous and lively. Our life was filled with happiness and vitality.

Our first mission field began in 1992, at the Betel Church, the first of many churches we pastored. Rafael was the lead pastor, and I supported him by staying by his side. The church was located in the village of Mandinga, in the Baracoa region, the easternmost part of Cuba.

One day, a brother from the church called Rafael. The man had found Elón in the church, playing with the

Christmas tree decorations. Rafa took Elón in his arms and explained the meaning of it all. Using words the child could understand, he told him about the birth and death of Jesus. He also mentioned the importance of giving our hearts to the Lord. They both ended up on their knees, praying together. At just two years old, Elón gave his heart to the Lord Jesus.

A few months later, we moved to Jibacoa, Manzanillo. At that time, Isaí was only five months old. There, we attended two churches, separated by five kilometers. That time lasted about five years. It was a precious time in which we saw God's hand in everything. Elón was a child very close to his family, who always said: «*Mommy, even if we struggle, we are together.*»

Isaí had been born with low defenses; he was a sickly baby. On one occasion, I was monitoring his breathing, and Elón approached me. He stood by my side and, with a pleading look, said: «*Mommy, look at me too!*» In that moment, I felt that God spoke to me. I understood that Elón also needed physical affection, hugs, and kisses. From that day on, each of them would have their own special place in my life. I then told them: «From now on, each of you will have one of my legs and one of my arms.» I can say with certainty that, from a very young age, Elón taught me how to be a better mother.

When he was five years old, I found him crying big tears. Alarmed, I asked him:

—Darling, what's wrong?

He replied:

—You don't love me.

Surprised, I asked with concern:

—What makes you think that?

—Because you don't talk to me —he lamented.

I tried to explain:

—Of course I will talk to you! Look, we're doing it right now.

Then his response disarmed me:

—Yes, but all you say is «Elón, come take a bath; Elón, come eat; Elón, don't do that.» That's what you talk to me about.

His words left me speechless. I understood that, although I was taking care of him, I wasn't dedicating enough time to talk to him and show him how much I loved him.

I apologized for neglecting something so important. We prayed together, and he asked God to help me become a better mom. When I asked him if he forgave me, he answered:

—Yes, mommy, I forgive you. Even pastors make mistakes.

I had to hold back a laugh at his sincerity. I thanked him, and from then on, every night we set aside time to talk about how his day had been. We also scheduled family meetings, often suggested by him, where we would evaluate the family's behavior. In these meetings, we would usually apologize to each other for not having been wise in certain situations.

Another custom we implemented in our home was not going to bed angry. Rafael and I taught them: «If Christ comes tonight for us, what will we say when we arrive in His presence?» That's why all problems had to be resolved before going to sleep. This gave meaning to the words of **Ephesians 4:26-27: «In your anger do not sin; do not let the sun go down while you are still angry, and do not give the devil a foothold.»**

Elón loved the Bible; he wanted to read it as many times as his dad. When I noticed, he was beginning to neglect this habit, I decided to write him a letter as if it had been sent by the Bible itself.

Elón and Isaí loved surprises. One thing we used to do was wake them up with a small gift. It could be an eraser, a pencil, a marker, or even framed photos of them with Bible verses. On this occasion, the surprise for Elón was a letter from his Bible, which said something like this:

«Elón, I am sad with you because I feel that you no longer love me as you did before; you no longer read

me as you used to. I want you to know how many wonderful things I have for you. Please, read me again. I love you very much. Your Bible.»

When he woke up, he said:

—Mom, do you think I'm stupid? The Bible can't write that. You did it!

—If she could write you a letter, it would probably look like the one in your hands —I replied.

God worked through the letter, and Elón resumed reading his Bible with such enthusiasm that he even asked his dad to buy him an alarm clock so he could wake up an hour earlier than usual. He wanted to read the Bible and pray at the beginning of the day. If he hadn't read it in the morning, during lunch he would say: «I can't eat what's material until I've been fed with what's spiritual.»

Elón wanted to be like his dad, a passionate follower of God's Word. He never stopped asking him how many times he had read the entire Bible; he wanted to catch up, at least by reading the New Testament. Before he went to heaven, he managed to read the New

Testament four times. His favorite books were Romans and Revelation.

We were a happy family. We shared life in harmony, playing and enjoying time together. Elón's creative ideas filled our home with joy. When he and his brother were restless and I would scold them, Elón would respond with liveliness:

—This is exactly what you asked us to do!

And in response, I would say:

—I overdid it.

Elón was a completely normal child. He played baseball, fought with other kids, and had fun with his little brother. Like any child, sometimes he had to be scolded, but often he would ask for forgiveness for his mistakes without anyone having to demand it.

It was also Elón's idea that, upon waking up, the greeting should be: «Lord, I love you. Daddy, I love you. Mommy, I love you. Isaí, I love you.» Each one had to follow the same formula, respecting the order of priority. Of course, we all had to start by putting the Lord first.

Elón was a generous boy. For example, of the four cookies he was given during school snack time, he always brought three homes: one for his dad, another for me, and the third for Isaí. He always made sure to bring his little brother's cookies so I wouldn't have to give him mine and be left without any. Even when we traveled with his dad, upon returning, he would have the cookies saved in his backpack. Although they were all crumbled to him, they were still ours, and he considered them sacred. That's why Jesus said:

«*Truly I tell you, unless you turn and become like children, you will never enter the kingdom of heaven*»

(Matthew 18:3).

I remember a special occasion. After putting the children to sleep and praying for them, I sat in a chair, watching them rest. At that moment, I felt the Lord speaking to me, saying:

—Tahimy, they are not bad. They are the best children in the world, despite the little time you give them.

Those words filled my heart. I immediately took a piece of paper and started drawing a diploma for each one. When my husband found out what I was doing, he said:

—If we're going to do this, let's do it right, with the home printer and colored paper.

And so we did. We printed the diplomas and placed them near the bunk bed where they slept. Since the wall dividing the bedrooms was made of sack, we put them at the top of the frame. The next day, Elón, who was the first to wake up, saw them and excitedly said to his brother:

—Look what they left us! It says we are the best children in the world, despite how badly we behave!

From the other room, Rafa and I listened to their conversation, trying to hold back our laughter.

Then Isaí responded:

—Well, you know, we can't fight anymore because they'll take the diplomas away from us.

Finally, I couldn't take it anymore and went to their room. I hugged them and said:

—No one is going to take that diploma away from you.

I told them that God had inspired me to make them and that, for us, they were the best children in the world. Rafa joined us, and together we explained that we weren't perfect parents, but they were wonderful. The diplomas stayed on the wall until we moved from that place.

The children loved evangelizing. They made a perfect duo: Isaí would start, and Elón would continue. I remember one time when they preached on a passenger truck. A young girl ended up crying, moved by the message. She couldn't understand how such small children could be so convinced of what they were talking about.

Elón would gather the neighborhood children and his classmates to take them to church, to **Sunday School**, and to the **Happy Hour**[1]. If anyone was absent, he would tell me:

—You see, Mom? The devil has him tangled up. If he dies, he's going to hell.

—Dear, we need to pray for them so that God can save them —I responded.

One day, he came home crying from school because the teacher had asked me to come. He had fought with a classmate, Juancito. I asked him to tell me the truth about what had happened, assuring him that I would trust him. He then explained in detail what had occurred. We prayed together and went to the school. After asking the teacher for permission, I spoke with the children in the classroom, and then with Elón and Juancito separately. After reconciling, Elón gave him a scented eraser as a "peace offering." To his surprise, Juancito gave him a ring in return, which Elón kept for a long time. The following Sunday, they were seen together at Sunday School, and they never fought again. They became great friends. Eternal friends, I have no doubt.

Elón was a very honest boy. When he came home from school, if he felt he had done something wrong, he would say:

—If you want to hit me, you can; if you want to scold me, you can; if you want to punish me, you can.

We always ended our conversations with a piece of advice and a prayer. One day, Isaí told me that his brother had danced at school and hadn't told me. When he realized he was caught, Elón exclaimed:

—¡Tattletale!

When I asked him if it was true, he said yes. Very seriously, I told him:

—God has a limit to His patience, and you can't play with Him.

Elón became thoughtful; his face showed that the idea was going around in his head. When his dad arrived, he asked:

—Dad, does God's patience have limits?

After talking to his dad, we spoke together using Psalm 1 as a basis. When we got to the part that mentions the chaff, he asked:

—What is the chaff?

After explaining it, we continued until we finished the passage. Then, he prayed and asked for forgiveness from the Lord, saying: "Father, forgive me for what I did. Help me not to be like the chaff, but like the tree planted by the streams of water, bearing the fruit of Your Spirit."

On another occasion, I was surprised that he didn't want to go to school, as he loved studying. When I asked him why he didn't want to go, he replied:

—I don't want to fall into temptation because this afternoon they're going to have a little party in the classroom.

Once, a young woman visited our house and mentioned that she didn't accept Jesus because she liked dancing too much. We tried to convince her, explaining that in some churches they dance for Christ, and that it wasn't wrong to dance for the Lord. While we spoke, Elón was paying close attention, his "radar" activated. When the young woman left, he began imitating the sound of a keyboard while dancing. Seeing this, I scolded him sharply. He mischievously responded:

—Mom, I was dancing for the Lord.

In our small house in Niquero, the children slept in bunk beds: Isaí on the bottom and Elón on top. Every night, I would accompany them to help them sleep. One of those nights, Isaí said worriedly:

—Mom, I'm not going to go to heaven because I fight too much with my brother.

Immediately, Elón responded:

—Well, I'm going to heaven because I have accepted Jesus as my only Savior. Now God doesn't see me for what I do or don't do; getting to heaven is only through Jesus. I am going to heaven!

Elón was a very diligent student. He didn't need to be told to study or do his homework; he did it on his own initiative. He was so reliable that the teachers entrusted him with the care of all the students' materials in the classroom. He was also very protective of his things. If his little brother Isaí touched something of his, he noticed immediately and would say:

—Mom, I know everything I have will be for Isaí, but please, let him leave it alone! I really want to live in a big house where he has his room and I have mine!

He loved animals. A sister from Las Coloradas, named Paquita, gave them two puppies: one for him and one for his brother. Elón named the male Skan, while Isaí chose the name for the female. Everything was going well until the puppies started getting into mischief. Their dad explained that we couldn't keep them because the yard of the house was the space we used as a temple for worship and meetings.

After deciding to give them away, the children and I cried a lot. I knew how much they meant to them, so I asked some brothers who lived nearby to take the puppies. This way, my children could visit them whenever they wanted. Since then, every dog that has lived at the home of those brothers has been named Skan, in honor of Elón's first puppy.

Elón's questions often surprised us, but one of his reflections deeply impacted me. One day, I saw him lying on his bed, staring at the ceiling with a worried expression. When I asked him what was wrong, he responded:

—Mom, have you thought about how difficult our life is? We can't have cats because they could hurt us, and we can't have dogs because there's no place to raise them. We also can't go to parties because it's a sin, or attend carnivals because they don't please God. Tell me, mom, when are they going to say yes to something for us?

That question, so profound for his age, made me reflect and have a conversation with his dad. We decided to accept a dog and find a place to raise it. That's how Pantera came into our home, becoming part of the family.

Elón took care of Pantera with great care. He would take her to the roof to prevent any dog, other than the one he chose from mating with her. He wanted to improve the breed, sell the puppies, and help his grandmother Loida financially.

—Since she's alone —he said—, I have to take care of supporting her, even if it's by raising puppies. But they have to be good dogs.

He loved his grandmother dearly. He would always tell me:

—You have my dad, Isaí, and me, but she's alone. Let's do something: I'll go live with grandma for a while to keep her company, or we can marry her off to some old man from the church.

Of course, I didn't accept his «proposals». And when a supposed suitor of my mom married another woman, Elón would say to his grandmother:

—See, grandma! By not listening to me, now you're alone again.

The goodbyes between them were always with tears. This is the last letter Elón wrote to his grandmother Loida:

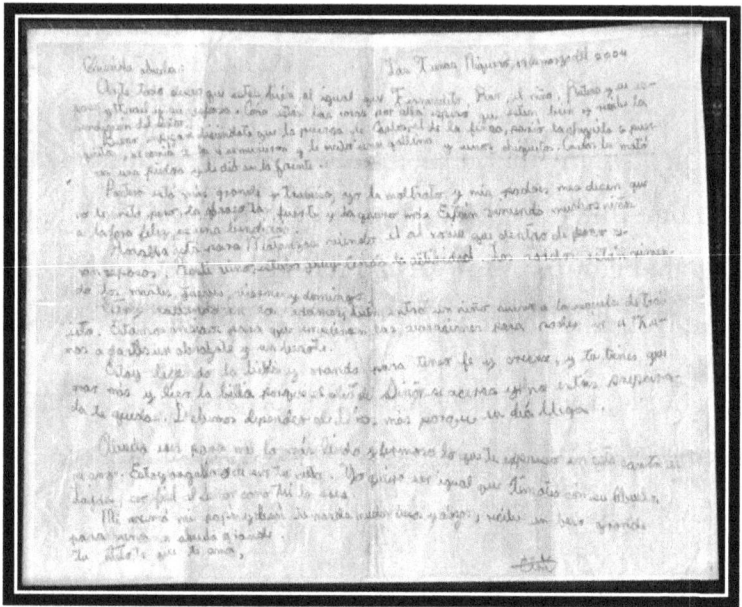

Las Tunas, Niquero, March 17, 2004.

Dear grandmother:

First of all, I hope you are well, as well as Fernandito, Rut, the child, Rutica and her husband, and Israel and his wife. How are things over there? I hope everything is fine, and may you receive the blessing of the Lord.

Well, I'll start by telling you that Carlos' little pig from the farm gave birth to six piglets; but she ate two of them, and the other four died. She also killed a chicken and some chicks. So Carlos killed her with a rock to the forehead.

Pantera is bigger and more mischievous. I mistreat her, and my parents tell me not to hit her, but I hug her so tightly and love her more.

A lot of children are coming to the Happy Hour, it is a blessing. Rosalba is in Matanzas visiting her boyfriend, who will soon be her husband. Rusty came, and the activity was really nice. The deaf are attending on Tuesdays, Thursdays, Fridays, and Sundays. I am doing well in the exams. A new child entered the driving school. We are excited for the vacations to come so we can go to Tunas and give you a big hug and kiss. I am reading the Bible and praying to have faith and grow. You also need to pray more and read the Bible because the day of the Lord is coming, and if you are not prepared, you will be left behind.

We must depend more on God, because His day is coming. Grandmother, you are the most beautiful and wonderful thing to me. What I express to you in this letter is my love. I am proud to be your grandson.

I want to be like Timothy with his grandmother Loida: to be faithful to the Lord like you are. My mom, my dad, and Isai send you many kisses and hugs.

Receive a big kiss for a great grandmother.

Your grandson who loves you,

Elón.

Elón was very close to his loved ones. For him, God and his family always came first. Every night, before going to bed, he included these words in his prayer:

«Lord, do not allow anything or anyone to separate us from You, nor each other.»

His personality left a mark on those around him. Teachers highlighted his imagination and the value he placed on family, faith, and study. On one occasion, I asked him:

—What has been the happiest day of your life?

Without hesitation, he answered:

—The day we went to Carenero beach.

We had gone as a family, the four of us together. We let them swim at the shore while Rafa and I chatted nearby. When it was time to get out of the water, we made up a game where we wrote phrases in the sand, and when the water erased them, it was a funny moment for them.

One of the things we taught our children was the scale of values. God first; then their dad, their mom, their little brother, and then everyone else. When they grew up and got married, their wives should come after God, and we, as parents, although deserving respect, should take the last place, as they would have a new family.

At nine years old, I found him lying on our bed, deep in thought. When I asked him what he was thinking about, he replied:

—About her.

A girl had already captured his heart. I will never forget when he told me:

—Mom, I'm in love. She is an only child and from Tunas, just like you. She's beautiful!

—Elón, do you love her a lot? —I asked.

With a romantic sigh, he replied:

—Look, mom, I love her so much that you are a little bit below her.

When we traveled to the United States with Rafa, Elón, with great selflessness, asked us not to bring him anything, but to get a gift for that girl, Masiel, his first love. Over time, I learned that Masiel, now eighteen, still thought about my son at night. She kept the gift he had given her in a special place. The young woman said that Elón had been the only man who truly loved her.

When Masiel confessed to me that she wanted to become a nun because she felt Elón's absence in her life, we had a conversation full of tears, a mixture of joy and sadness. I then asked her from the bottom of my heart to give me the grandchildren that Elón would never be able to give me.

To Elón, we, his parents, were perfect. His dad was a champion, and I was the most beautiful woman in the world and the best cook; and the best part was that I believed it. One day he told me that he wanted to marry a woman who wasn't «dry».

—That's easy —I exclaimed laughing—. If the girl is dry, you just throw two or three buckets of water on her, and problem solved.

We all laughed, happily.

On some occasions, when he saw me serious, he would say:

—Mom, you're letting yourself be tempted by the enemy.

—If I keep laughing, my teeth will get cold from having them out so much —I would respond.

His greatest satisfaction was seeing his parents kiss or hug each other. He also showed happiness when Rafa gave me flowers. If several days passed without him noticing any affectionate gesture, he would push me to his dad and say:

—Dad, give mom a kiss, you're forgetting!

I always wore makeup and took care of my appearance from morning to night. If for any reason I didn't, the first to notice was Elón, who would say:

—Mom, you're letting yourself go.

The church was far from the pastoral house, and we only had one bike. The children preferred to run so that I could ride with their dad, making sure I didn't have to walk.

Often, Elón would sit me in a chair and say:

—Mom, you are the queen of this home. Now Isaí and I will take care of everything.

One would clean the yard, and the other would help inside the house. Everything was spotless, although, without them realizing, I would go behind them, fixing little details. When we traveled, the three of them would take care of the suitcases and even my handbag, because according to Elón: «We are the gentlemen, and you are the lady, and ladies shouldn't get dirty.» If we went out and I took a little longer talking to someone, Rafael and Isaí would walk ahead, but Elón would always wait for me. At those moments, he would say:

—I won't leave you behind because I'm your man, and I have to take care of you.

When Isaí would arrive late from school, Elón would scold me as if it were his responsibility:

—What kind of mother is this, not worrying about her son! Look, mom, all Isaí's classmates have passed, and he's still not here.

I would ask him to calm down, assuring him that his brother would be there in a few minutes. And indeed, that's what happened. Elón would wait at the door, welcoming Isaí as if he were his father.

I remember a little neighbor, whom I'll call Pedrito, a four-year-old boy who didn't know how to express affection. I discovered this when, when asking for a kiss, he only offered his cheek, and when I hugged him, his little arms stayed stiff. I taught him how to give kisses and hugs, and from then on, every morning he would come to our house to receive these signs of love.

One of those mornings, Elón, jealous, asked me:

—Why does he get it, and I don't?

—Don't be unfair —I scolded him—. I carry, hug, and kiss you and your brother every day. But he doesn't have parents, and he probably lacks affection.

Elón quickly replied:

—In my school, there are many kids whose moms and dads don't hug or kiss them. If I bring them here, will you do the same as with Pedrito?

I never imagined that that same afternoon, when returning from school, he would come back with a line of children. I sat them on my lap, hugged them, and one by one told them I loved them.

One of the children Elón knew was going through a very difficult situation. So, one day he asked me for permission to give him some of his clothes. I told him to pick whatever he wanted to give. To my surprise, he chose the best clothes: shirts, socks, underwear... I had no choice but to praise him from the bottom of my heart for his generosity.

Many times, he would come with a group of kids at lunchtime, and since I hadn't planned for it, I would end up without food. I would then explain to him that he needed to give me advance notice so the food wouldn't run out. But he would reply:

—It's just that my friends like your food because their parents' food tastes old.

At other times, after eating, he would say:

—Mom, the food was delicious; you're the best cook. But today I'm not hungry.

That's when I would realize, humorously, that my food that day also tasted «old».

Elón was incredibly affectionate. To express what I meant in his life, it never seemed like he had enough time. He would show his love almost every five minutes. Every now and then, he would run through the door, wrap his little arms around me, and say:

—My queen, my princess, there is no woman more beautiful than you.

He would repeat it so many times a day that I ended up believing it. I will never forget his magical words, the ones that always made me feel reborn:

—Mom, you know I love you so much! Do you know that, mom?

—My love, I know you love me, and I love you even more —I would reply.

When he saw me cry, he would ask, worried:

—What's wrong? Did my dad do something to you?

He would ask because he heard his friends talk about how some dads mistreated their moms. With a smile on my face, I would reply:

—No, my love, nothing is wrong between us; your dad hugged me today. It's just that women, when we get older, sometimes feel like crying, and we can't stop. Elón, when you get married and something like that happens to your wife, you just have to hug her and say, "You know you can count on me." Then you'll see how, little by little, she'll feel better.

Elón stayed still for a few seconds, thinking. Then he looked at me, and as always, he gave me a hug and asked:

—Mom, do you know that I love you?

And he added:

—I know what you're going through. You can count on me —and he kissed me and went off to play.

Our lives seemed calm, but in my heart, there was an unsettling anxiety. I felt that something was about to change, that our lives would never be the same.

LITTLE DIAMONDS

Chapter 2
AN UNFORGETTABLE FAREWELL

On April 2, 2004, a boy came running and told me:

—Pastora, Isaí fell from a tree; he's on the ground and can't get up.

I ran immediately to the place. I found him almost unconscious; I tried to revive him, but he was only vomiting. I feared the worst. My prayer at that moment was: «God, I don't ask you to take him or leave him; let your will be done. But whatever it is, give me strength.»

We took him to the hospital in Niquero, where he was quickly referred to Bayamo. The neurologist diagnosed a concussion; his cerebellum was so affected that it took two days for him to walk again, and when he did, he had difficulty with coordination. Over time, he improved, and in less than fifteen days, he was walking normally. Thank God!

Finally, they discharged him, and we returned to Niquero. We arrived at night, but even so, Elón and Isaí talked until dawn, as if they were two friends who hadn't seen each other for a long time and had a lot to share. Elón said to me:

—Mom, don't you realize that Isaí is a better brother after the fall?

God, who makes all things perfect, granted them fifteen days of peace and tranquility between them. On Friday, April 30, I was sitting in the living room when Elón ran to my lap. Isaí tried to take over, but I explained that for fifteen days, he had both my arms and legs all to himself. I asked him to share them with his brother for a while. Isaí agreed and went off to play. At that moment, Elón said to me:

—Mom, if you and I are walking down a path, and a car comes speeding and hits me right in front of your eyes, what do you do?

—Elón, don't be dramatic —I replied—. That's never going to happen.

But he insisted:

—Mom, if you and I are walking down a street, and a car comes speeding and hits me right in front of you, kills me, and you can't do anything for me, what do you do?

—I'll push you so that it hits me and not you.

He didn't give up:

—Mom, the car is speeding, hits me, and you can't save me, what do you do?

—I'll scream so loudly that my screams will be heard all the way to Havana.

With a mischievous laugh, Elón replied:

—No, Mom, you don't need to scream, because you know where I'm going.

Two days before that conversation, he had been repeating this verse:

«At home, everyone cries because the pastor's son has died.»

Every time I heard it, I asked him not to repeat it, because those words hurt me so much.

After holding him in my arms for a while, I went to finish the meal. He followed me and asked:

—Mom, wouldn't you like to fly?

—Not by plane, because I'm afraid of it.

—I don't mean flying by plane, Mom, I mean flying, flying, and flying...

Later, I served the meal. We only had three small steaks that had been given to us. I saved them for them. I never knew how Elón figured it out, but after finishing his meal, he handed me his plate and said:

—You know, I liked the rice so much that I didn't want to eat the meat. I'd rather you eat it, but in front of me.

And I, like an obedient child, ate it. That night, Elón couldn't fall asleep. He woke up around midnight and didn't sleep again. I spent the whole night talking to him, praying, petting him, and reminding him how much we loved him. After 4:30 in the morning, he finally fell asleep. At 5, I returned to my bed, where Rafael was lying, who had also not been able to sleep.

I took a biblical promise: «And God will wipe away every tear from their eyes, and there will be no more death».

On Saturday, May 1, at seven in the morning, Elón called us as usual:

—Lord, I love you; Daddy, I love you; Mommy, I love you; Isaí, I love you.

After this greeting, Elón told his dad that the clock had stopped. That same day, his heart would also stop beating.

A while later, a group of teenagers came to pick up Elón and Isaí to go to Carenero Beach. The noise of the young people prevented me from hearing what Elón was saying until I heard his shout:

—Mommy!

When I reached him, he looked at me with his big, beautiful eyes. Then he apologized for having hurt me and, once again, uttered his magic words:

—Mommy, do you know that I love you very much? Mommy, I love you very much!

Before leaving for the beach, he asked me to pray for them. After the prayer, I went out to say goodbye to them. However, at that moment, Isaí decided to stay. Then Elón approached and said to me:

—It's better that Isaí doesn't go because something might happen to him.

Then he gave me a kiss, a hug, and left.

The counselor accompanying the group told us that, before heading to the beach, Elón prayed again. Once at the beach, they talked and made a pact with God. In his prayer, Elón said: «Lord, I ask you to keep me pure and clean for you and for the young woman you have for me».

On returning from the beach, Elón approached his counselor and asked:

—Why don't you come with me to my house and ask my parents' permission to let us stay tonight praying in the temple?

She replied that his parents already knew and agreed. However, instead of going straight home, Elón went to ask the parents of one of his best friends to let him stay in the temple. On the way, they started bouncing their ball, which ended up hitting a tree and rolling into the road. Since he was so careful with his things, he didn't want a car to damage the ball. He immediately went to retrieve it, and suddenly, a truck hit him. That's how God took him to heaven.

Meanwhile, Isaí was at a friend's house who also hadn't wanted to go to the beach. We were at the Methodist church, where we had gone to look for the books "Dare to Discipline" and "How to Raise Boys." While we were talking about the books, I felt a pang in my heart, jumped in my seat, and exclaimed:

—Oh, Rafa, Elón!

Rafael tried to calm me down:

—Don't worry, he's probably fine and already on his way back from the beach.

But I insisted so much that we decided to return home. On the way, we saw a crowd of people. The rumor was that a child had been killed. In my heart, I knew it was Elón. Not finding him at home, we went to the accident site. There were his shoes, his ball, his backpack, and some flip-flops that weren't his. A sister from the church tried to convince me it wasn't Elón, assuring me she would have recognized him. However, I knew my son had a blue backpack and a ball. Everything matched.

To be sure, we needed to go to the hospital. Rafael didn't want me to accompany him, but I managed to get on the back of the bicycle without him noticing. Upon arriving at the hospital, the crowd was such that we could barely enter. Rafael went to the morgue. I didn't have the courage to accompany him. After identifying himself as the father of one of the children who had been playing with the ball, they allowed him to enter.

Later, he told me that, as he approached and observed the covered body, he only needed to see one of his toes to recognize him. It wasn't necessary to look at his face to know it was him.

He went on to say

What else did we need? Comfort! But not that of the policemen who were waiting around the body waiting for a reaction from the relatives against the person responsible for the accident.

«*My help comes from the Lord, who made heaven and earth*».

«*He will not fear bad news; his heart is steadfast, trusting in the Lord. His heart is secure; he will not fear...*».

—All eyes were on me, waiting to see if I would scream in hysteria or react with vengeance. I'm not sure to what extent our silence became fuel for others. It's true that it hurt us, and we still wish he were with us.

He came out and confirmed what I feared the most: it was our son, Elón. We held each other, crying. I felt like I was losing all human strength. On the way back home, I kept telling everyone I came across, «*It was Elón, it was Elón who was killed*».

When we arrived, the house was full. I don't remember the number of people gathered there; some were familiar, others were not. Everyone wanted to share our grief. The neighbors were crying... We decided not to postpone the inevitable and broke the sad news to Isaí that his brother had died. He couldn't understand and said to me:

—Mami, don't cry. He'll come back. I was in the hospital too, and look at me here.

—Isaí, God's plan isn't the same for everyone —I said—. The Lord wanted to take your brother and chose to leave you. He knows why.

But Isaí insisted:

—Mami, do you remember the story of Lazarus, Jesus' friend? That's what's going to happen. God can bring him back to life. He's not dead; he's just at the hospital and will come home in a little while.

With my heart shattered, I explained:

—Isaí, your brother is with the Lord, and that's a truth we cannot change.

We spent nearly an hour trying to help him understand.

With time, our son Isaí wrote:

> «It was for that very reason that I didn't get angry with God when He took my brother. I didn't have, don't have, and never will have the right to question Him. I didn't understand why he had died until my mom explained it to me so clearly that I finally got it. If my brother had survived, maybe he would have strayed from God's path. I'm sure the Lord saved him from something worse. It's time for you to give it a try, even if no one close to you has died like in my case. If you want some advice: love and protect your loved ones, because later you might regret it. I'm speaking from experience. Just as it happened to me, it has happened to many people who, unlike me, sought refuge in vengeance instead of in the infinite love of Jesus.»

AN UNFORGETTABLE FAREWELL

When Yordy Toranzo, the pastor of the Methodist church, heard the news, he couldn't believe it. He reacted by hitting the wall and crying out to the Lord, asking why this had happened to us. Both he and his wife wept for our son and took charge of all the funeral arrangements. We will never forget the love and support we received that day.

As we waited for the body to arrive, I approached a group of brothers and sisters gathered nearby and said:

—Until now, God has given me strength, but I need more to see my son in a coffin.

Pastor Yordy suggested to Rafa and me that we kneel down and cry out to the Lord, assuring us that He would answer. So we did. During the prayer, I had a vision: hands wearing what appeared to be white gloves, holding us as we floated upon them. When we stood up, we felt such strength that some people began to judge me, saying I didn't love my son. Others remarked on how strong we were. But Rafa and I knew that strength wasn't ours; it came directly from the throne of God. His power multiplied through the prayers of brothers and sisters around the world who were interceding for our family.

That night, when it was time for Isaí to go to bed, I walked him to a neighbor's house. I will always be grateful to her for the way she cared for my son. My children loved her deeply and affectionately called her «Queta.» Still outside, I knelt down, hugged Isaí, and asked if we could pray together before he went to sleep. We did. After a goodnight kiss and a «*God bless you,*» Isaí turned to me and said:

—Mom, I don't want you to cry anymore. Do you see the sadness we're experiencing because of Elón's death? That's nothing compared to the blessing God is going to give us—not just up in heaven, where Elón is already rejoicing, but also here on Earth.

Hearing this revelation from my nine-year-old son, I hugged him again and replied:

—Son, may God hear you!

—Mommy, believe it, because it will happen!

Due to legal procedures, Elón's body took a while to arrive. Finally, it entered the church in Niquero around two in the morning. That was one of the hardest moments of our story. Rafa uncovered the casket, and I showered his body with kisses, just as I had done so many times when he was alive. His hands, now lifeless, would never again hold me on this earth. His body was bruised, and he had a large wound on his head. There lay our son, our great Elón. I ran my hands over his arms and said to the Lord: «*When no one remembers him anymore, he will live in my heart forever. My beloved son, my Great Man of God.*»

With the arrival of morning, pastors from all over began to gather to support us. Cars filled with brothers and sisters from various churches arrived to join us. At that moment, I remembered how, when Elón was alive, he used to tell me: «*The day I die, please hold a service with lots of singing.*»

We talked so much about heaven with our children that they didn't see death as something grim but rather as a way to draw closer to God. They would tell me they wanted to meet Jesus face to face and, if He allowed, sit on His lap, hug Him, and kiss Him. When we spoke about eternity, I often explained it using a blank sheet of paper. I would put a tiny dot on the paper and tell them that was how our life compared to eternity: nothing. The important thing was to secure our life with Christ. This teaching resonated so deeply with Elón that he began sharing it with his classmates.

The church was packed. There were people who had never been there before, and their presence represented an opportunity that couldn't be wasted. I approached several brothers to ask them to lead the funeral service, but all of them, through tears, said they couldn't do it. Then I thought: *«Lord, if You have given me the responsibility of speaking about You to people I don't know, give me the strength to do it once more, now in front of my son's body.»*

My legs were shaking, but I began:

—This morning, we are not holding a service for a dead person, but we wish that those who do not know the Lord have the opportunity to hear about Him. *We say as Job did: «The Lord gave, the Lord took away; blessed be the name of the Lord.»*

I spoke about what Elón had asked me before he died: a service with songs and praises to God. And so it was. The service started in the morning and finished in the afternoon, with eight different messages from the pastors. At one point, Pastor Francisco Álvarez came up to me and said that it was too much for me, that I should let him help. We continued together. We sang several of Elón's favorite songs: «*God is in control of all things, yes*», «*The Mighty One of Israel*», and «*The Victorious lives in me*». Rafael wanted to preach the last message using Elón's Bible and some passages he had marked. While he spoke, we saw tears in the eyes of everyone present. However, we were convinced that no one had taken our son from us; it was the Lord who wanted to take him. God had lent him to us; he bElónged completely to Him. This certainty calmed my soul: my son was in the presence of the Lord, just as he had longed for. Elón had learned to love his Heavenly Father deeply, and he was sure that love was mutual.

Isaí asked his father to let him go to his brother's funeral for a little while because he wanted to see him one last time here on earth. Rafael took him. He stood by Elón's casket, firm like a little soldier. After a while, he said:

—Dad, take me home because this is too hard for me.

Then began the hardest task: facing two dead children, one physically, and the other emotionally. Only the grace of God could help us overcome this new stage in our lives.

This is how Rafael referred to that period:

«When our son left and went ahead to the Heavenly Glory, it was a violent, disorienting blow. I went silent. All the plans and dreams I had with him collapsed. I thought he would close my eyes. What a disappointment: I was the one who had to close his.»

"For none of us lives to himself, and none of us dies to himself."

I am not able to know to what degree Elón was able to grasp this concept, but these are some of his notes, written when he was only eight years old:

«It all started preaching the word of God, because it changed my life, it made it new. And now I preach to Him, because He saved me from the destruction and decay of sin.

One day, I sinned in church and had an experience with Him. And the greatest experience I can have with Him is to go with Him.»

«I am in third grade, preaching to my teacher; I am winning him for Christ. Even though sometimes I can't stand my parents, I continue with my ministry and stay firm in God. I write this because I want to remember this experience with the Lord when I am an adult, that is, a teenager. Also, since my experience has been sad, I want someone to accept Christ as their Savior and Lord. Please, accept Christ and give Him your soul for when the great tribulation comes. I do not bElóng to myself; I bElóng to Jesus. I give my life for Him because He saved me from destruction.»

Pastor Francisco Alvarez Cantillo dismissed the mourning using the words said to David:

« *Your chair will be empty, and you will be missed.* ».

This has been the case. Elón's teacher had to change classrooms and schools because he couldn't bear to see his empty seat. Our son's life deeply moved the people of Niquero, and his death did as well.

In Cuba, where we lived, it is customary to exhume a person's remains two years after their death. In our case, that time was extended to three years because, due to Isaí's physical and emotional health, we moved to Bayamo. Those three years passed quickly. The time had come to take our son's remains from the grave that a brother had lent us. Many warned me that, being physically weak, even epileptic, something could happen to me. But I replied to all of them:

—In truth, I am not strong, and I am at a disadvantage compared to other women, but I know that Christ lives in me, and that is enough.

Some brothers, even pastors, expressed their interest in accompanying us. But only Rafael, Verónica (a little friend of Elón), the brother who drove the bike taxi to transport the remains, and among us, the Lord as our Mighty Giant, came. The gravediggers were expectant about what could happen. While they were breaking the lid of our son's grave, I said to my Father: « *Father, please, give me strength.*». And He gave it to me, against all human expectations. The Word of God became real in my heart once again: **Where, O death, is your sting? Where, O grave, is your victory?... But thanks be to God, who gives us the victory through our Lord Jesus Christ»**

(1 Corinthians 15:54-57).

After the exhumation, I experienced the joy of the resurrection. I asked those present for permission to pray, and they all, in unison, said yes. But before doing so, I had the opportunity to preach to them about the Lord. I carried the small box with my son's bones, and it was as if I was holding him in my arms again. I felt an inexplicable joy in my heart; a desire to cry out to the world, like those women at the empty tomb of Jesus:

«*He is not here, but has risen*».

No matter how much I explained, no one could understand what I felt. It was as if, from heaven, the Lord and Elón were looking at me, smiling and telling me that the most precious part of him was with Jesus.

The next day, we moved Elón's remains to Bayamo. Rafael and the Lord accompanied me to the necropolis. His little bones were still dirty, and since Elón was so neat, we cleaned every part of his body with great care. We powdered and perfumed him. For this, we chose the best of our napkins and divided it in half. Rafa cleaned his head, and I cleaned the rest of his body. Then, we placed him in a niche that we know God chose for him. When we finished this act, I felt in my heart: «*It is finished.*» I had completed the task with my son, the son that God had lent me."

One day after Elón's death, I had a conversation with God:

—Lord, I don't question You because I know he didn't bElóng to me. I don't want You to get angry with me, but why did You lend him to me and take him away so quickly?

And I added:

—Lord, You don't have to answer me because You are sovereign.

But He, in His mercy, spoke to my heart as He had done many times before:

—Some entertained angels in their homes without knowing it. I lent you an angel for eleven years, and you didn't know.

On another occasion, Isaí asked me:

—Mom, why did God take my brother?

My mother, who was at home, replied:

—Because the Lord needed him in heaven.

However, Isaí was not satisfied with that answer, and he retorted:

—With so many children in heaven, why did God want another one? The one who needs him is me, here on earth.

These and other questions filled his mind. His short age didn't allow him to fully understand what was happening, but we kept trying to give him answers that he could comprehend.

One year after Elón's death, Juancito, his friend, along with several of his classmates, asked their parents for money to have a snack after the May Day parade. To everyone's surprise, instead of food, the children bought a bouquet of flowers and took it to Elón's grave. There, they told him about their feats, such as the home run that allowed them to win a baseball game. They also told him how much they missed him.

Many judged us because they didn't understand how we could sing next to our son's coffin. But despite everything, we are deeply grateful to the people in general because we know they truly loved our little one. First and foremost, we thank God because Elón's life testimony led many people out of darkness to know Christ. This was the case of Sister Fabiola Picado, who gave her life to the Lord after hearing Elón's story. She currently serves as a missionary in North Carolina. Today we can clearly see that God does not make mistakes. Elón was, is, and will always be a blessing to our family.

AN UNFORGETTABLE FAREWELL

Miss me but let me go

When I reach the end of my journey
and the sun no longer shines
I don't want rites in a melancholic room
Why cry for a liberated soul?
Miss me a little
but not for too long
and not with your head bowed
Remember the love we once shared
This is a journey we all must take
and each must go alone
It's all part of the Creator's plan
a step on the path to home
When you're alone and distressed
seek the friends we knew
and bury your sorrows with good deeds
Miss me, but let me go.

Unknown author

Chapter 3
THE STAGES OF BEREAVEMENT OF A LOVED ONE

I would like to share with you the different stages of grief and some practical tips that have helped our family cope with separation. Our desire is to help you through the stages of grief, regardless of the order in which they occur.

Over the years, I have learned that no matter how hard we try, it is impossible to avoid grief. In fact, trying to do so may be a manifestation of the «*denial*» stage (we will talk about each stage later). In reality, we have to face it, go through that process.

We also cannot expect those who have not suffered the loss of a child to fully understand us, even if they respect our pain. That said, it is important to acknowledge that every type of loss has its impact and value.

Grief manifests itself in a unique and personal way. In my experience, I have seen that sometimes a hug, a cup of coffee, or any other gesture of kindness at the right moment is worth more than a thousand words. Someone once said: «*Do not be afraid to share your story; you never know if it might be the key to unlocking someone else's door, or even their prison*».

On one occasion, a person said something that made me reflect:

«*What do you call someone who has lost his or her husband or wife? Widow or widower.*

And someone who has lost his or her parents? An orphan. But what do you call someone who has lost a child? He or she has no name ».

That is how indescribable the pain we experience can be. However, every pain matters, and we all, when facing a loss of any kind, need to go through our stages of grief.

In 1969, Swiss-American psychologist Elisabeth Kübler-Ross developed a model to describe the stages humans go through after losing a loved one. These are known as «*the five stages of grief*»: **denial, anger, bargaining, depression, and acceptance.**

- **Denial:** It can't be!
- **Anger:** Why is this happening to me?
- **Bargaining:** I would do anything to change this situation.
- **Depression:** Why continue after this loss?
- **Acceptance:** It's going to be okay.

According to Kübler-Ross, grief depends on each individual's personality. Some people may go through these stages in six months or a year, but when the relationship with the loved one is very close, the process can extend to two years or more. If denial persists for long periods, it is advisable to seek help from a specialist.

Grief can manifest in different ways and at different times. According to psychotherapist Cate Masheder, who works with people who have experienced grief, the starting point for accepting loss is to recognize death and the resulting pain as something natural. Masheder states: «*Death is part of life. It's going to happen. We are all going to feel sadness; we are all going to miss someone; we are all going to die. That's how it is*».

Masheder uses a visual explanation to describe the impact of grief. On a piece of paper, he draws a circle representing the person and says:

«*Imagine that this is you, and everything that has to do with your life is inside this circle.* ».

Then start coloring the circle, explaining:

« *When grief comes, there is not a single area of your life that is not affected by that pain. It reaches every part of you* ».

He goes on to explain that it was once believed that the pain of bereavement diminished over time. However, it is now understood that this is not the case:

« *The current approach is that this pain remains as it is, but our life grows around it*».

According to this perspective, we do not overcome pain, but learn to integrate it and allow it to be part of our life.

The denial stage: No way!

Experts explain that denial can initially serve to cushion the impact of the death of a loved one, delaying some of the grief. However, this stage cannot last indefinitely because, eventually, reality sets in.

During denial, we find it difficult to assimilate what has happened. Personally, I believe that it is a defense mechanism that God has put in us to process the loss little by little. For example, there are people who, after losing someone, try to continue with their lives as if nothing had happened. However, sometimes it is enough to come across personal objects of the person who is no longer with us to activate repressed memories and feelings.

This attempt to repress the pain may last longer or shorter, but the truth will confront us sooner or later, and we cannot help but recognize it.

Fortunately, the stages of grief do not follow a strict order or have a definite time frame. Acceptance will come when you are ready to receive it.

The anger stage: Why is it happening to me?

During the anger stage it is common to experience feelings of rage, resentment and even hatred. The search for those responsible or to blame may also arise. Anger appears as a reaction to the realization that death is irreversible, which generates deep frustration. This anger can be projected towards the environment, affecting close people who are also going through their own grief. Such an attitude can be harmful and complicate relationships with those who try to offer support.

Most of the time it is not possible to prepare for the loss. Therefore, anger can lead us to act in a way that impacts those watching us. While it is understandable to react by yelling or punching a wall, what is not acceptable is to take action against those around us. We should not yell at them, blame them or direct any kind of abuse toward them.

If you feel you cannot control yourself, ask for help. You don't necessarily need to go to a licensed psychologist or professional therapist; it can be a good friend, a pastor or an older person you trust. The important thing is to prevent your pain from causing further damage.

Remember that those who love you understand that you are going through a difficult situation, but it is not fair to abuse them.

The negotiation stage: I would do anything to change this situation.

During this stage, it is common to fantasize about the idea of having prevented death. Many people ask themselves, «*What if...?*», or think of strategies that could have avoided the final outcome, such as, «*What if I had done this or that?*».

Do not dwell on such thoughts, as you will never find answers to those kinds of questions. Neither the past nor the future belongs to us. We can only change the present. If you do not focus on the here and now, you risk turning the present into the «*What if...?*» of tomorrow.

In this regard, I am particularly struck by an expression from Pastor Dante Gebel: «*God does not say "I was" or "I will be"; He is the "I am" in your life.*»

The Lord wants to be the God of your present, the one who walks with you and gives you strength TODAY.

In the New Testament, the Bible tells the story of two sisters, Mary and Martha, who lost their brother Lazarus. When Jesus came to them, they said to Him: **«If you had been here, my brother would not have died»**

(John, Chapter 11).

Although much has been preached about this miracle, the moving detail that **«Jesus wept» (John 11:35)** is rarely reflected upon. Seeing the sisters' suffering, He shared their pain.

Be certain that your pain is also God's pain. It is normal to try to negotiate with Him or question His plan, but rest assured that God understands you and does not hold your words against you. He is with you, even in your moments of greatest fragility.

The depression stage: Why continue after this loss?

Every good therapist will explain that deep sadness and a sense of emptiness are typical of this stage. We are not talking about clinical depression, which is a mental health issue, but rather a set of natural emotions tied to the pain caused by losing a loved one.

During this stage, some people may feel they have no incentive to keep living and choose to isolate themselves from their surroundings. Let me ask you: Are you still breathing? Are you alive? Do you have someone to live for? If you believe there is no one, then live for yourself! Remember, your story can shine a light for those facing a situation like yours.

If it had been the other way around, how would you want your child to react? Would you want to see them without the will to live? Or would you prefer that they face life bravely, seeking help to overcome your absence?

If we could ask our children who are no longer with us and they could respond, they would surely tell us: «Keep moving forward! That is what you taught me. Be strong! I want you to live!».

Today, at this moment, do you exist or live? I invite you to reflect on this. It is not the same thing to exist as to live, and I want to give you good news: the God in whom I believe says in his Word, which is the Bible:

«I have come that they may have life, and have it to the full»

(John 10:10-11).

Only the Author of life can restore to you the desire to live, not just to exist. There is a big difference between the two.

When you feel like you're falling into depression, do not reject those who seek to be with you. The company of your loved ones can be the best medicine. From the experience of a friend who suffers from clinical depression, I know that when you fall into deep sadness, the only thing you want is to be alone. But that isolation only feeds the depression. This causes dangerously low levels of serotonin and dopamine in the brain, and these decreases intensify when facing the loss of someone you love. This scenario becomes fertile ground for the enemy of souls: the devil.

I would like to tell you that there is a method or a medicine to ease your pain. However, over time I have come to understand that only Jesus Christ can heal such a pain. I bring all my broken pieces to Him, and He puts them back together.

Do you want to find peace? Let me tell you that peace is not a circumstance, but a person, and that person is named Jesus. His Word reminds us that He is the Prince of Peace: «*For to us a child is born, to us a son is given, and the government will be on His shoulders. And He will be called Wonderful Counselor, Mighty God, Everlasting Father, Prince of Peace*».

(Isaiah 9:6).

Jesus says:

« My peace I leave with you, my peace I give you; not as the world gives do I give it to

you. Let not your heart be troubled, neither let it be afraid. Believe in God, believe also in me.»

(John 14:27).

He also says:

«And the peace of God, which transcends all understanding, will guard your hearts and your minds in Christ Jesus»

(Philippians 4:6-7).

The acceptance stage: It's going to be fine.

According to the definition from the Royal Spanish Academy, accept is a transitive verb that means «*to receive voluntarily or without opposition what is given*». It is «*to agree to something*».

Once the loss has been accepted, bereaved people begin to learn to live with their emotional pain in a world where the loved one is gone. Over time, they regain their ability to function, to experience joy and to find pleasure in things again.

From the perspective of a servant of God and father of my children, Pastor Rafael Tamayo explains:

"Assimilating pain is not the work of a day or two; it takes time, and also spending time with God. We had to ask for pastoral leave because our family was devastated. Needless to say, it was unexpected. Let us weep in Christ who gives us true comfort, true peace in the midst of the storm; He gives us victory, in Him we can trust. Recover your courage with me, though our past is gloomy and our present suffocating, the brightness of our trophy is visible in the future.

About the five stages of grief

Grief does not follow a specific form or order; it manifests differently in each person, as we are all unique. The fact that the reactions to pain are more visible in some people than in others does not mean their love for the lost loved one is any more or less deep.

According to experts, not everyone goes through each stage of grief. It also does not follow a specific order in all cases. These stages may appear at different times, in varied sequences, or even repeat. This will depend on the individual and their personal process.

When does grief become a problem?

Are there only five stages, or are there more?

Some psychologists consider that grief can encompass seven stages. In addition to the five stages we have mentioned (denial, anger, bargaining, depression, and acceptance), two more stages are added: confusion and guilt. These two additional stages can appear at any point in the process.

The confusion stage

«The confusion that arises can lead to a feeling of great anger and resentment. The person may even blame the rest of the world and themselves because they believe the situation is unfair.»

It is common that, in the midst of grief, some people become angry with God. If this is your case, I remind you that the Lord Jesus understands you and does not criticize you. He knows your heart and understands how much a mother or father can suffer from the absence of their child.

God tells us in His Word:

«Will a woman forget what she has borne, so that she will no longer pity the child of her womb? Even if she forgets, I will never forget you.»

(Isaiah 49:15).

God knows that it is impossible to forget a child. That is why, in this process, He wants to be your help.

In the book of Job, the Bible tells the story of a righteous man, pleasing to God, who lost all his descendants in one day: seven sons and three daughters. He also lost his health and his wealth. Can you imagine how much pain his heart and his wife's heart must have felt?

In his despair, his wife said to him: «*Curse God and die*».

We could judge her, but God did not. He understood her pain and granted her seven other sons and three daughters.

This shows that a person's thoughts or words spoken in the midst of their suffering do not offend God. He understands your pain and knows how you feel. The

Lord will not only be with you on the good days, but also (and especially) on the bad days, in those moments when you see no way out.

The guilt stage

During grief, the feeling of guilt is inevitable. Although we know we cannot prevent death, many people feel guilty for not having spent more time or for not having expressed their love better to the deceased. It is normal to think that there were things left unsaid.

In these cases, you need to ask God for forgiveness and, symbolically, ask forgiveness from the one you lost. But, most importantly, you need to learn to forgive yourself. You cannot go through life carrying guilt. Forgiveness sets us free. That is why you should start by forgiving yourself.

After the death of our son, a close friend, Onilda Cervantes Maristany, connected us with a psychologist.

The doctor asked me:

—What hurts you the most about Elón's death?

—That I wasn't the mother he deserved —I replied.

Quickly, the doctor called other mothers who were nearby and asked them the same question. All of them admitted not being satisfied with the mother they were.

We are not taught how to be a mother or a father. That is why it is important to forgive ourselves constantly. This becomes easier when we repent and ask for forgiveness before God.

Different forms of parental grief

Not all parents experience grief in the same way. Reactions may be similar to other losses, but are often more intense and prolonged when a child is involved.

Here are some of the most common reactions:

- Intense trauma, confusion, rejection and denial, even when her son's death was expected.

- Overwhelming sadness, to the point that performing daily tasks or simply getting out of bed seems impossible.

- Extreme guilt, accompanied by the feeling of having failed as a protector and that I could have done something different.

- Intense anger and bitterness, with the feeling that the child's life was not fulfilled.
- Fear of being alone, which can lead to overprotection of living children.
- Resentment towards parents with healthy children.
- Feeling of existential emptiness; life seems meaningless. Often, there is a desire to be united with the deceased child in order to be free of grief.
- Questioning of faith or loss of faith.
- Dreaming of the deceased child or feeling his or her presence.
- Loneliness and intense isolation, even when surrounded by people; there is a feeling that no one can really understand their grief.

How children and teenagers understand death

When a child passes away, parents are often the focus of attention. However, an important question arises:

What about the grief of siblings?

They, too, have lost an important part of their life: their companion, their confidant, their soul mate.

My son, Isaí, wrote on a piece of paper:

> «Elon, my brother, there is no one like you. I have wanted to fill your emptiness with my cousins and friends, but every day I realize that this wound, this great pain that I have, no one can fill it, only God and time.».

Tips to help siblings cope with grief

So how can we help our children cope with this loss?

Some psychologists suggest the following:

- Make bereavement a shared family experience.
- Include children in conversations and plans to honor the deceased sibling.
- Spend time together, talking about their sibling or doing activities.
- Make sure children understand that they are not responsible for their sibling's death.

This will help free them from feelings of guilt and remorse.

In our experience, Jesse felt great guilt. He came to think that he was responsible for his brother's death. He often said, "If I had gone, my brother would not have died; it would have been me instead."

We had a hard time removing this idea from his mind, but with the Lord's help we were able to get him to understand that no one was to blame. We explained that Elon's death was part of God's plan for his life.

It is important to remember that each individual is unique and special in his or her own way. comparing a deceased child with a survivor can generate feelings of injustice and pressure on the living child. it is essential to avoid making comparisons and instead celebrate the unique qualities of each of them. each person deserves to be recognized for his or her own virtues and to be valued for what he or she brings to our lives.

Let your child know that you don't expect him or her to fill the void of the one who left.

Once, we told Isaí:

—You are the child we love the most.

—I'm the only one left —he replied.

Then, we took that moment to tell him a story from when he was a baby. I was paying attention to his breathing, and Elón caught my attention, saying:

—Look at me too, mommy.

We also shared other similar anecdotes, which I believe marked the beginning of his emotional healing.

- **Establish reasonable behavioral limits.**

It is important to find a balance between not being overly protective and not being overly permissive.

- **Ask a close friend or family member for help.**

If your own grief does not allow you to give them the attention and love they need, a loved one can be a great support.

Helping yourself through grief

Pain is inevitable, but these suggestions can help you cope with it in a more bearable way:

- **Talk frequently about your child and pronounce his or her name.**

Talking about Elon and mentioning his name helped me a lot to cope with my pain. Almost twenty years have passed and I still mention his name every day. I learned not to cry for his death, but to thank God for his life and for the time I had him with me.

- **Ask for help from family and friends.**

Allow them to help you with household chores, errands or caring for your other children. This will give you time to think, remember and process your grief.

- **Take your time to decide what to do with your child's belongings.**

Don't feel pressured to pack his things or give away his toys or clothes. We took our time deciding who to give Elon's belongings to. We also saved a few things for Jesse, since he is younger and we could put him to good use.

- **Be prepared to answer difficult questions or uncomfortable comments.**

Questions like «How many children do you have?» or comments like «At least you have other children» can be difficult. Remember that, in most cases, they don't intend to hurt you; they just don't know what to say.

In my case, I usually respond: «I had two children. One is named Elón and is with God; the other is Isaí, and he is still with us.»

This allows me to affirm that both will always be our children, regardless of whether they are physically with us or not.

- **Plan how you want to spend your significant days.**

Dates such as your child's birthday or the anniversary of his or her death can be emotionally challenging. Decide ahead of time how you want to deal with them.

In my experience, I usually spend the anniversary of Elon's departure in isolation and sometimes fasting. But I do so not from depression, but from prayer and gratitude. I thank God for the time he granted me with my son.

Near his birthday, we met in the Families with Hope ministry. I will talk more about this ministry in the next Chapter.

- **- Keep his/her memory alive.**

You can spend these days looking at photos, sharing memories or starting a family tradition, such as planting flowers. Experts recommend these practices because they are healthy and help keep good memories alive. Remembering the good things about the one who is gone is a way to keep him or her present in your life.

- **Seek support from a support group.**

Parental grief is very intense and often leads to isolation. Therefore, it may be beneficial to attend a support group where you can share your experiences with other parents who have gone through the same thing. They will understand your pain. In our case, as a family, we found refuge by meeting with other parents who have also lost children. This experience was key to our healing.

THE STAGES OF BEREAVEMENT OF A LOVED ONE

"The footprints"

One night in a dream I saw

That with Jesus I walked

By the seashore

Under a silver moon

I dreamed that I saw in the skies

My life represented

In a series of scenes

That I silently contemplated

Two pairs of firm footprints

In the sand they were leaving

While with Jesus I walked

Like friends conversing

He looked attentively at those footprints
Reflected in the sky,
But something strange I observed
And I felt great dismay

I observed that sometimes
When I looked at the footprints
Instead of seeing the two pairs
I saw only one pair of them

And I also observed
That that one pair of footprints
Were mostly observed
In my starless nights

In the hours of my life
Full of anguish and sadness,
When the soul needs
More comfort and strength

THE STAGES OF BEREAVEMENT OF A LOVED ONE

I sadly asked Jesus:

Lord, hast Thou promised us

That in my starless nights

You would always be with me?

But I note with sadness

That in the midst of my quarrels,

When I feel the suffering the most,

I see only a pair of footprints

Where are the other two,

That indicate your company

When the storm lashes

My life mercilessly?

And Jesus answered me

With tenderness and compassion:

"Listen well, my son,

I understand your confusion:

A BORROWED ANGEL

I always loved you and I will love you

And in your hours of pain

I will always be by your side

To show you my love

More, if you see only two footprints

In the sand as you walk

And you don't see the other two

That should be noticed

It is that in your afflicted hour

When your steps falter

There are no traces of your footsteps

For I carry you in my arms.

THE STAGES OF BEREAVEMENT OF A LOVED ONE

Chapter 4
TURNING OUR SORROWS INTO STRENGTHS

The loss of a child marks a before and after in our lives. The sadness can envelop us in such a way that, sometimes, we don't even recognize it. Often, the circumstances and the expectations of others prevent us from expressing the depth of our suffering. After the passing of our son Elón, we faced an even greater challenge: the deep sadness of our second son, Isaí. A psychologist told us at that time: «You have two dead children, one physically and the other emotionally». That phrase resonated in our souls.

To begin transforming our sadness into strength, we first need to recognize our vulnerability to pain. I remember one of those days when the pain was so intense that I felt I couldn't bear it anymore. I fell to my knees crying out to God for peace and comfort. In the midst of my suffering, I became very studious of God's Word. I began writing letters to the Lord, pouring all my anguish and pain into a notebook.

One of those endless sleepless nights, while I thought about what our life would be like from that moment on, the idea came to my heart to write a book that would capture our story. Maybe this would help other parents going through similar pain. This book was initially written by Isaí, my husband, and me. Later, upon arriving in the United States, I worked on a second edition, which is the one you are reading now. I share this because sharing our pain with God and expressing it in writing was fundamental to our healing process.

I know that if you turn to Him and trust Him with your sadness, He will listen to you and understand you. After all, God Himself experienced the pain of losing His son on the cross, Jesus Christ, out of love for you and me. He understands us like no one else can.

It is common to share our sadness with people who, although they love us, cannot understand our pain.

This happened to me: I shared my story with some people hoping to be heard and understood, but in many cases, I found only expressions of pity or indifference. I don't judge them, because they simply couldn't walk in my shoes.

An unexpected call

Around 2004, shortly after losing Elón, we were asked to comfort another family who had just lost their three-year-old son. Our friends thought that, as parents who had lived through the same experience, we could be a source of strength. The truth is that I felt completely powerless. What words could I offer to someone experiencing such deep pain? The idea of facing another grieving mother terrified me. I felt like a leaf in the wind, unable to find the right words.

When the first person came to find me, I simply said «no».

A second person came, and although I wanted to refuse again, I thought, «Maybe the Lord wants me to go speak with her.» So I proposed the following: «Let's go to your house. If she wants to talk to me, I'll be ready;

but if she prefers her space, we will respect that.» To my surprise, shortly after, she sent for me. I didn't know what to say, so I prayed, «Lord, give me the right words to help this young woman.»

During our conversation, an idea arose that would change my life: to form a support group for mothers who had lost their children. I explained to her that no one could understand our pain like we could, because we had lived it ourselves.

When I returned home, crying for my son and for hers, my husband wisely told me that perhaps I wasn't ready to take on that commitment. However, over time, I understood that sharing my pain with other mothers would be the key to turning my sorrow into strength.

It wasn't until 2017 that I took the first step to turn my pain into hope. That year, we organized the first meeting of Women with Hope at my house. Only Clara Vivian attended, a mother who had lost her only daughter, Eliza, at the age of twenty-three.

Clara's story deeply moved me. As I listened to the details of Eliza's illness, I couldn't help but remember my own loss and cry for Elón. When she finished telling her story, Clara said to me: «I was able to do everything for my daughter, but you couldn't do anything for yours.» Both of us understood, in God's mercy, that she had the opportunity to accompany her daughter until the end, while the Lord spared me from seeing Elón suffer.

Clara was the first to experience the healing and hope our group offered. Seeing her transformation, her husband, Ornel, wanted to be part of the process and began accompanying her to our meetings. That's when we decided to change the name to Families with Hope. This way, we included all those who, like Ornel, were seeking support and healing. Today, Clara and Ornel are the national leaders of our movement in Cuba, opening doors to new families across the country.

All glory to God for this wonderful work.

I want to share with you another moving testimony. It is about the case of Juanita and Guicho, a couple very dear to us. They had only one daughter. The girl was born healthy, but over time she developed serious health problems. She reached a point where she could neither speak nor walk; she couldn't lead a normal life like other children. Her parents never had the joy of hearing the magical words «mom» and «dad». However, their love for her made them happy during the thirteen years they had her. After losing their daughter, the words of **Psalm 32:3** resonated deeply in their hearts: **«While I kept silent, my bones grew old through my groaning all the day long.»**

The silence of those around them only worsened their pain. However, when they came to Families with Hope, they found a safe space where they were listened to and could share their experiences. By doing so, they strengthened their faith and became a source of comfort for others. Our dear brothers told us that the hugs they could never receive from their daughter, they found in our group.

Today, Juanita and Guicho lead Families with Hope in Baire, Cuba. They have turned their trial into a platform of help for other people who have yet to be restored.

Another moving story is that of Marta, a woman who, after years of longing for a child, finally got to embrace her little one. Unfortunately, tragedy cut her life short when she was fifteen. Marta learned about the existence of the Families with Hope group and came to see us. We never pressure anyone to share their stories until they are ready, and it took a long time before our dear Marta could share her experience. She had to leave the town where she lived because it was too painful for her and her husband to stay there. After many years, she returned to Baire, not to mourn the death of her daughter, but to help console others. Today, she is a leader in another part of Cuba, Sibanicu, and also in Camagüey.

Gisela, a mother who had lost her child in an accident, came to our group devastated. We shared her pain and cried together. At a moment of deep sadness, Gisela said, «I'm making a hole here and I'll bury my sorrow.» Later, when we were more comfortable, I said to her: «Why didn't you make that hole in the street?» We all laughed, but that was the beginning of a restoration. Today, Gisela is an indefatigable leader in Bayamo and

Victorino, demonstrating that even in the darkest moments, we can find light and hope.

Dianelis' story reminds us that the pain of losing a child, no matter their age, is a deep wound that's hard to heal. Her first child had died when very small; but for a mother, this doesn't matter, because it's always about our children. Dianelis came to our group very sad, carrying her second child in her arms, but still unhealed from the goodbye to the first. We all embraced her and cried with her. After attending the group for some time, we asked her what Families with Hope meant to her.

Dianelis replied:

«When I arrived, I thought I would never be able to laugh again, but thanks to God, today I can do so freely.»

I could keep sharing countless stories of pain and healing, but I believe the most important thing is to recognize that each of these experiences is unique and valuable. By sharing our stories, we not only find comfort but also inspire others to find their own path to healing. And it is in this spirit of solidarity that I want to talk to you now about something that has been fundamental to our healing: our faith in Jesus Christ.

If you notice, we all have a common denominator: the same pain and the search for a solution to our sorrow. I would like to tell you that there is something magical in all of this, but that's not the case. People like me have found comfort and strength in Jesus Christ. We have given Him our fears and our failures. You may be wondering, «Why the failures?» Well, after the death of your child, you might feel that you have failed as a parent, that you didn't do enough for them. But I want to tell you something: even if you had them in your arms, they would still leave you. We have no power over life or death; that belongs to God. However, in the midst of our pain, we have discovered an invaluable treasure: hope. I know that we are not prepared to say goodbye to our children, but we cannot change the situation. However, we can think and ask ourselves some questions, for example: «Do I have life?» which is not the same as simply existing. In this regard, I have good news for you. The Bible says: «The thief comes only to steal, kill and destroy; I have come that they may have life and have it in abundance.» He can return to us the life that the enemy of our souls has stolen from us: joy and peace are precious treasures that the Lord wants to restore, along with the desire to continue living. And it is in this hope that we find the strength to move forward, rebuild our lives, and find a new purpose.

The other question is, «What do I want to do in the face of the physical death of my child: remember the experience of separation or thank God for the time and blessing of having had him by my side?» I chose the second option. I thank God for Elón's life in our lives; he made me a mother, and my husband a father. Even if it had been just for one day, it would have been worth it. Every moment by his side was a gift, a treasure we will always keep in our hearts.

I can understand that, many times, you feel without strength and with no desire to go on. There are moments when it seems like your heart is in pieces. However, that is the exact moment to give all those broken pieces to the only one who can put them back together: God.

When I think about this, I remember a dynamic we did in the group. I asked Brother Pablo to prepare a puzzle in the shape of a heart with many pieces. After presenting it to the group, we gave ourselves five minutes to assemble it together. As expected, we didn't manage to do it; it was too difficult, and the pieces were too many. In the next meeting, Brother Pablo presented the puzzle already assembled. When showing it, I explained: «Only the person who created it could put it back together.»

That's how it happens with our broken hearts. Only He, the great Artist of life, can take our pieces and create a work of art, even if the cracks remain.

A love letter from God

After Elon's departure, we found in his Bible several verses that, at the time, were like a love letter from God to us. One of them said:

«And the peace of God, which surpasses all understanding, will guard your hearts and your minds in Christ Jesus»

(Philippians 4:7, NKJV).

I want you to notice something important: in this verse, God mentions two essential parts:

- The heart, where we feel the pain.
- The thoughts, where a constant battle is fought.

In my most intense moments of grief, I would tell God:

«*Dad, it hurts, your daughter Tahimy hurts so much.*»

And something incredible was happening: His peace and comfort were coming into my life. It was as if God, knowing the depth of my pain, whispered to me: «*Daughter, I am with you, and my peace will surround you.*»

If you allow God to draw near to your pain, that peace will also come into your life.

Another of the precious pearls we found among Elón's things was this verse:

«*In Christ Jesus, we are more than conquerors*»

(*Romans 8:37, NKJV*).

We cannot overcome the anguish, pain or torment of separation in our own strength. Therefore, Jesus reminds us that only in Him are we more than conquerors. This verse became our shield and our sword in the battle against pain.

A revealing dream

Before the death of our son, I had a revealing dream. I was in a hallway between the house and the fence, with several dogs on top of me. Upon looking at them closely, I realized they were not just animals, but demons.

In the midst of the struggle, someone handed me a sword which I held firmly. I saw myself lifting it so high that it reached the sky. Then, I shouted with all my strength: «In Christ Jesus, we are more than conquerors!».

In that moment, all the animals fled, and an army of angels appeared before me. Immediately, we joined our voices and began to sing:

«In Christ Jesus, we are more than conquerors!».

I woke up with a mixture of emotions. I had never dreamed of angels or demons before. But that dream confirmed to me that God gives us the necessary tools to overcome any battle, no matter how great it may seem.

When I found Romans 8:37 highlighted in his Bible, I understood that the multitude of angels in the dream represented the people who had been praying for us. It was then that the Lord showed me the transforming power of prayer. I realized that those prayers ascended like a cry to heaven, and that God, in His infinite mercy, had answered them.

After sharing our experience and walking this path of pain and healing, we want to leave you with some reflections that we hope will serve as a guide:

- **Gratitude and hope:** thank God for the time shared with your child and for the opportunity to have been their father or mother. Faith is a fundamental pillar in this grieving process, as it gives us hope for the future.

- **Connection and solidarity:** seek support from grieving communities or people who have gone through similar experiences. Sharing your feelings and experiences will help you feel less alone and find comfort in connecting with others.

- **Sharing and healing:** don't be afraid to tell your story. By sharing your pain, you can help others feel understood and find their own path to healing. Remember: in giving, we also receive.

- **Forgiving and moving forward:** if you feel you have failed in some way, ask God for forgiveness and forgive yourself. Forgiveness is liberating and will allow you to move forward in your healing process.

- **Learning to live with the pain:** pain is an inevitable part of life, but we can learn to live with it in a healthier way. Turning pain into a driving force to help others can be a way to give it new meaning.

- **Seeking help:** don't hesitate to seek professional, family, or spiritual help. God is close to the brokenhearted and can provide you with the comfort you need.

- **Giving purpose to the pain:** ask God how you can honor the memory of your child and help others through your experience. Your pain can become a force for positive change in the world.

- **Channeling pain into love:** use your pain to love others. The world needs more love and compassion, and you can be an instrument of God to bring that light to others.

Remember the following:

- Faith in God is a balm for the soul.
- Community is a safe haven. Do not isolate yourself
- Sharing your story is an act of courage and love.
- Forgiveness sets you free.
- Pain can be transformed into purpose.
- Love is the answer to everything.

- Your experience can be a source of inspiration and hope for many people. Don't hesitate to share your story and seek the support you need.

«The Lord is near to the brokenhearted and saves those who are crushed in spirit.»

Psalm 34:18

TURNING OUR SORROWS INTO STRENGTHS

A borrowed angel

On March 18th

an angel was heard singing

from the sky.

Her voice was so sweet

that nothing could compare.

On earth, everyone wonders:

«Where is that sound coming from?»

Only one person answers:

«That's me, dear mom.»

Her mother, moved,

doesn't know whether to laugh or cry,

and thanks God

for such immense goodness.

The days fly by,

some come and others go,

and in a small house,

peace and happiness reign.

«Who will live in that little house

with so much humility?

Could it be that an angel came down from heaven

to live in it?»

She makes everyone so happy,

but the hard part comes when she leaves.

Perhaps the whole family

will burst into tears.

A BORROWED ANGEL

Goodbyes are sad,

and this one is harder than the rest,

because the angel returned to heaven

and nothing could be done.

Only one comfort remains:

they will be able to go home

to be united once more

for all eternity.

In heaven, we don't know

what other name Jesus will give her,

but I do know that on earth,

Elón, Elón, will always be.

Bibliography

BBC Mundo. (2018, April 26). Cuáles son las 5 fases del duelo y por qué no es algo que necesariamente tienes que dejar atrás. BBC News Mundo. Retrieved from https://www.bbc.com

American Society of Clinical Oncology. (2019, September 13). Grief after the loss of a child. Cancer.Net. Retrieved from https://www.cancer.net

Asistea, Grupo ASISTEA. (2019, October 29). The stages of grief after the death of a loved one. ASISTEA. Retrieved from https://www.asistea.com

Sociedades Bíblicas Unidas. (1960). Santa Biblia, Reina-Valera 1960. Madrid: Sociedades Bíblicas Unidas.

Sociedades Bíblicas Unidas. (2011). Santa Biblia, Nueva Versión Internacional. Miami: Sociedades Bíblicas Unidas.

Schwiebert, P., & DeKlyen, C. (n.d.). Sopa de lágrimas: Receta para sanar después de una pérdida.

Made in the USA
Columbia, SC
25 February 2025